# House Churches
*Back to the Blueprint*

Copyright © 2019-20 Yowza Publishing
All rights reserved.

Cover Image from
Wokandapix from Pixabay

First Printing: 0 9 8 7 6 5 4 3
ISBN: 978-1-951410-10-0

Yowza Publishing

# House Churches
## *Back to the Blueprint*

"A Pentecostal Paradigm"

As demonstrated by the New Testament's early church.

By Linda Jones

# DEDICATION

*To all the brave souls who are not afraid to buck tradition and to my son Bradley for helping me get this into the hands of "the new reformers."*

# CONTENTS

| | | |
|---|---|---|
| 1 | Why a House Church? | 1 |
| 2 | Are House Churches Scriptural? | 7 |
| 3 | A Look at Some Early Ministry | 17 |
| 4 | Called and Gifted Leaders | 27 |
| 5 | Nine Gifts of the Spirit | 37 |
| 6 | Having Church in a New Testament Manner | 57 |
| 7 | A Meeting in a Home | 65 |
| 8 | Women in the Church | 69 |
| 9 | Some Church History | 71 |
| | An Outline on Becoming a Christian | 79 |
| | An Outline: for Receiving the Holy Spirit Baptism | 81 |
| | Twenty-nine Evangelism Ideas | 85 |

Linda Jones

# CHAPTER ONE
# WHY A HOUSE CHURCH?

The calling of the church is to see the kingdom of God expand and be an expression of the kingdom of God on earth. (Matthew 6:10) Today many believers have a desire to fulfill that plan. Basically, they want to be used by the Lord spiritually when they go to church and not just be a spectator. Iron sharpens iron, and we need to receive encouragement and inspiration from each other in order to reach our cities for the Lord.

There are some Pentecostal churches that have cell groups in homes that fulfill the need for relationships and ministry in the Holy Spirit. It is certainly possible to have a home meeting and belong to a denominational church. There are individual house churches that are associated with other house church bodies. I am writing this book because I believe we all need to be in a biblical form of fellowship if we really want to experience the results of the New Testament first century church.

Jesus said, "Whoever desires to come after Me, let him deny himself, and take up his cross and follow me. For whoever desires to save his life will lose it, but whoever loses his life for my sake and the gospels will save it. For what will it profit a man if he gains the whole world, and loses his own soul?" (Mark 8:34, 35) There is a need for today's serious disciples to be involved in something more than what is usually offered on Sunday mornings!

All too often today's Christians in America do not study the word for themselves. They do not participate in inter-action when they attend a church service, and all too often they never discuss the word of God with anyone else. That is part of the reason many are leaving church and many others are hungering for a new paradigm to live out their spiritual relationship with other believers. There are many who desire to see miracles today in the church like happened in the Book of Acts. If they have been a Christ follower for very many years, they know there needs to be a better way than the church is experiencing!

There are many believers who have a rich experience with the Lord in their homes as they worship and study the word for themselves, but I find it hard to believe that there should not also be a hunger to get together with others in the body of Christ for spiritual fellowship. There should be a desire to want to encourage other believers through sharing the word together. There are some Pentecostal churches that have rich altar services where they minister to one another under an anointing but let us not limit what God's word shows us is available.

There are those who would say today's culture is too different from the one in Jesus day for us to do church as demonstrated in the New Testament. There is absolutely no way we can take the Bible and make an intellectual debate out of the historical issues and come up with something that makes the church in the Book of Acts exclusive for only the first century. We can't start tearing pages out of the Bible because we do not do church that way today!

Jesus called the common man to come and follow

him, and for two millenniums there have been pockets of Christians who have lived out the book of Acts in their culture. The church in America is missing the mark when it comes to maintaining a Christian culture, and it could be because the paradigm and the focus of the church world has changed from the original blueprint in the Word of God.

We have many church growth programs, and we have developed mega churches, but we have not turned the world upside down as the early church did. A move of God must be organic. By that I mean God wants to build his church! I was on the front lines of the Charismatic Renewal that spread the last real world-wide move of the Spirit. Home groups came together through the leading of the Holy Spirit, and it was in these gatherings that we learned to move in the gifts of the Spirit.

### *The Shepherding Movement*

That movement of home meetings faded away by something called "The Shepherding Movement." Pastors discouraged their people from attending anything that wasn't under the traditional church auspices. Leadership in the body of Christ, including home meetings, must lead by example, not control. As one person put it, bad leadership uses intimidation and manipulation to lead to domination. Jesus was not intimidated by the Pharisees, because he knew what the word said, and he obeyed his Father. It takes that focus to go against traditions that would stop obedience to what the Bible clearly teaches.

People want to be loved. We all need to be recognized and have friends. God the Father desired a family. He is called our Father! We need to see the people in the body of Christ as family. We are created to have a relationship with God and other believers. It is God's plan.

No group, friendship or marriage will know intimacy unless people seek both to know and be known. We should care when someone goes to the hospital or when their child sick. We are composed of spirit, soul, and body and the church is comprised of people who have families, homes and careers. God created planet earth for us to live out a plan that glorifies him and represents his kingdom. He cares about the hairs on our head and all the details of our lives!

*Different Types of Gatherings*

The body of Christ should manifest a "lifestyle" as the church. We should not compartmentalize our lives as secular and spiritual when it comes to relationships. The life of the church encompasses all of life, not just church services! We want people to desire to come together. Believers should have different types of gatherings to include different teaching gifts, music gifts, etc. In other words, think outside the box, and you will find the Holy Spirit may give some real soul winning inspiration as well as good times of fellowship and growth. Leaders give fluctuation to people in their attendance because control does not bring heart obedience.

This book is a Pentecostal book, because the book of Acts and the early church is a Pentecostal movement. Stick with the Bible!! Judge all things by scripture. Holiness is not legalism, and your example will lead people into holiness quicker than the law. A good thing about home meetings is that peer pressure works! We have influence on those with whom we are in contact. Like family, we desire to please those we are close to and our faith will encourage one another. We tend to be like those we hang out with, and true believers hang out with Jesus.

Invite people. They will come! Do not expect people to quit their church because they come to your house church or home meeting. Do not compete with anything going on in the body of Christ. Let the Lord take care of leading people. Again, people will go where they are being fed. People will commit to being faithful as they grow in their relationships with the Lord and each other.

People are desperate for real connection with other believers who are hungry for God! I pray the Lord will lead you to practice hospitality and open your home up. I pray a network of house churches will spring out of your home fellowship. It is time to take our cities for God!

I am not going to address baptism, church membership, tithing, etc. We are just going to focus on getting people together where they can grow in their relationships with the Lord and each other centered around their faith in Christ.

## CHAPTER TWO
# ARE HOUSE CHURCHES SCRIPTURAL?

Is a church in the home Scriptural? We see the formation of the New Testament church in the book of Acts. We observe the followers of Jesus gathering in Jerusalem in prayer waiting for the promise of the Holy Spirit on the day of Pentecost. They met in a large upper room, and Bible scholars believe it could have been the home of Mary who was the mother of John Mark. They deduce this because John Mark was a protegee of Peter, and Peter spent time with believers in that home. A hundred and twenty were in prayer when the Holy Spirit was poured out on the day of Pentecost! The church was born meeting in a large home! If we desire God's plan for the church, we must go to the New Testament for direction.

In the Book of Acts, we read that new believers met in various homes. In Revelation the letters to the churches were addressed to various cities in the Roman province of Asia. There were several house churches in each of these cities, and they passed the letters from church to church, and often town to town. The churches were to be unified not divided into sects. The Apostle Paul corrects the Corinthian church in I Corinthians chapters 1 and 3 against division.

In Mark 7:13, we are warned to beware of traditions that void the commandment of God. In Colossians the Apostle Paul says, "Beware lest anyone cheat you through philosophy and empty deceit, according to the tradition of men according to the basic principles of the world, and not according to Christ." All tradition is not wrong, and all the contemporary church traditions are not wrong, but the overall denominational and independent church structures are not patterned after the New Testament.

The church meetings in America operate more like the service in a Jewish synagogue than the book of Acts. This book is written for Pentecostal believers. However, evangelical believers like Francis Chan can see the need for spiritual relationship among believers, and he was willing to divide his mega church into small groups so the body of Christ could have more interaction and be used by the Holy Spirit.

A preacher who preaches salvation relies on a supernatural act for a person to be born again. It is my prayer that all true believers in Jesus will open their understanding and their will to all the supernatural ministry promised to the church through the Holy Spirit.

Willow Creek Community Church, a mega-church, stated they have gone from a church with small groups to becoming a church of small groups. Before this, only ten to fifteen percent of their people were connected. They realized that community was something a lot of people talked about, but few did anything about it. Leadership must have a vision to develop other people's ministry.

In China we see a movement of house churches because the registered churches are controlled by the communist government. Many westerners can't understand why people can't just conform when the government seems to be putting a stamp of approval on registered churches, but many believers desire the freedom to worship as they please and are not open to allowing government intrusion. The government in some providences turns a blind eye to home churches. In others they must remain underground to avoid being persecuted, sent to jail or worse. In fact, even as I am writing this, persecution has escalated for Chinese Christians. (We need to thank the Lord for the freedoms in this country and take advantage of them.)

Three gospels have a story about putting new wine in old wineskins. "No one sews a piece of unshrunk cloth on an old garment, or else the new piece pulls away from the old and the tear is made worse, and no one puts new wine into old wineskins or else the new wine burst the wineskins, the wine is spilled, and the wineskins are ruined. But new wine must be put into new wineskins." It wasn't long after Jesus ascended that the early Christians were persecuted by the Jews and could no longer attend the temple publicly. They were forced to meet in homes and give up the temple worship. In 70 AD the temple was destroyed, and the Jews met in synagogues exclusively. We know that as the apostles preached in the synagogues it usually brought division and persecution and the true believers in Christ began to meet in homes.

Paul's epistles were written to correct and encourage Christians who met in homes. He taught them to have church in a way that was different from the Jewish structure. The old wineskin, the Jewish traditions, did not allow for the moving of the Holy Spirit as we see in the New Testament Church.

Dr. David Yonggi Cho does church growth

seminars around the globe, because he has the largest church in the world having reached over a million people in South Korea. He has spent many years emphasizing the importance of cell groups. I watched a seminar done several years ago in London where he explained that his church had 50,000 deacons. These were cell group leaders leading a meeting in their home. These Deacons, of which two-thirds were women, won people to the Lord and then discipled them in their home. This is how he grew such a large church. He had 600 Associate pastors who had oversite over the cell groups. He had 1400 elders. He preaches to the people on Sunday and the church provides what he considers the cell groups covering. This isn't exactly how I see church designed in the Bible, but the cell group model has the heart of the gospel in getting people involved!

I Corinthians 1, Paul addresses divisions in the Corinth church. Stay humble and do not be like the group in Corinth who thought they were doing church better than others and became exclusive. That is what has caused denominational division in the body of Christ today. If what we are doing works, others may follow and get involved.

The world will know we are Christians by our love for Jesus and one another. Satan knows he can divide and conquer. In John 17 Jesus prayed that we would all be one as he and the Father are one. This should be our desire and goal. The Holy Spirit moves where we have unity of purpose and heart. However, sometimes there must be division when truth is more important than maintaining peace. Jesus taught us we must love him even more than family.

# CHAPTER THREE
# A LOOK AT SOME EARLY MINISTRY

We will look at life and ministry in the early church and see how we can apply it to a group of believers who meet today.

The first business of the church we see in the Book of Acts takes place after the ascension and before the Holy Spirit is poured out on the Day of Pentecost. (Acts 1) The believers were of one accord in prayer when Peter stood up in the midst and said they needed to replace Judas with another Apostle. They wanted to choose someone who had accompanied them all the time the Lord Jesus went in and out among them from the time of John the Baptist until the resurrection. They proposed two: Justus and Matthias. They prayed for the Lord to show which should be chosen, cast lots and it fell to Matthias. It is interesting that they chose Matthias in the presence of all the believers. It was not done in private. People join a home group because they want to be included when plans are made that affect the group. It is good to remember this.

After Pentecost the believers continued steadfastly in the Apostles doctrine and fellowship, in breaking of bread and in prayers. (Acts 2:42-47) The believers had all things in common and spent time together. They were willing to sell their possession and goods and divide them among all as anyone had need. This brought them much favor, joy, and the Lord added to the church daily those who were saved. Their giving was voluntary not mandatory.

The church in the Book of Acts was obviously more relational than the church often is today. God is relational. He desires a family. Jesus said, we are to abide in Him, and His Word is to abide in us. He calls us to oneness with Him and with each other! (John 17) We are called the children of God. God is our Father. We are called to be brothers and sisters in the Lord.

The first century, early church did not live in communes like the hippies of the sixties. They owned their own homes. Some were wealthy, some were poor, but they cared for one another. They also, did not become a socialist society where they are forced to all be the same economically. We learn to walk in unity by living to please the Lord. If we love our brethren, we will obey His commands. (I John 5:2) Our unity is centered around our relationship with the Lord.

We live in a covetous generation in America. All of society, and the church too, often judges people according to what they own. The Bible calls this a major sin! (James 2:2) It seems like a paradox that God desires to prosper His people, and yet the Word tells us that covetous people should not be appointed to leadership. (I Timothy 3:3) We need to remember that it is the love of money that is evil, not money itself. We also need to know that the church should share with those in need. I believe our first responsibility is to those in our fellowship, not the unsaved. I say that even though much of my ministry has been as co-director of homeless shelters. All of humankind is important and valuable, but the church is admonished to care for the brethren who are in need, and true religion is to care for the widows and orphans of the church. The advantage of a house church is you can really know the needs of those among you in a way that a traditional church may not. We want to minister to the whole person.

We see Ananias and Sapphira punished by the Holy Spirit. They were not forced to give more than they wanted to the Apostles. They lied about what they were giving, and it was punished by death. WOW! Great fear came upon the church. True believers are hungry for truth! It seems like extreme punishment to us today, but we need to learn from the reaction of the Holy Spirit about the seriousness of lying to church leadership or anyone else. (Acts 5)

### *Word of God Must be Taught/Preached/Shared*

It is important to remember that the anointed preaching of the Word is what brings change and hope. Jesus preached good news to the poor. Rev. David Yonggi Cho of South Korea has seen many millionaires as well as other members come out of the extreme poverty of South Korea through good preaching!

A house church should be formed to develop body ministry. It should never be a preaching platform for one person. A certain teacher may preach but that should not be the paradigm for every gathering.

People participating in a home church movement must remember that the life of the church is a volunteer movement. We are called to serve one another out of a grateful heart. God calls people, but He doesn't force anyone to accept Him. We lead by example. When we stand before the judgment seat of Christ, we should be like Paul, who boasted that his crown was the brothers and sisters who eagerly looked for the return of Jesus. (Philippians 4:1) We are called to edify and bless one another. Life can be creative or restrictive, but when we commit our way to the Lord, He promises to direct our paths. When we commit our work to the Lord, He promises to direct our thoughts. God is a God of order, but do not restrict the life of the church to always be the same. Let the creative dreams flow. Every believer is a part of the body of Christ has a ministry and function.

At first the early church centered around Jerusalem, and this lasted until persecution came. During this time, we see Peter and John arrested. However, the power of the Holy Spirit kept the church strong and they did not compromise with the world. They continued to preach daily in the temple and from house to house. They determined to obey God rather than man. They were passionate and bold. No work of God will succeed without passion. Trials and persecution will come, but victory is yours in Christ Jesus.

*Structure is Needed*

The first century Jerusalem church needed more structure with the increase in new believers, so they chose seven deacons to do the hands-on social ministry to free up the Apostles to preach and teach. However, these Spirit-filled deacons also preached the gospel in power and demonstration of the Spirit. Steven, a deacon, became the first martyr. He was taken before a Jewish council and was stoned to death. However, at his trial he was able to preach the gospel in fullness to them. He preached the plan of God for Israel beginning with Abraham and ending with the cross. Stick to the message! Our goal is to equip every believer with a knowledge of the Word. (Ephesians 4:12) We also are bold in the face of persecution and rejoice that we are counted worthy to face various trials for our faith. (James 1:2)

### *Foundation of Apostles and Prophets*

The first ministry officers we read about are the apostles. After Jesus ascended and the Holy Spirit was poured out, they began new churches and helped to correct problems that arose in the churches. When Jesus was on earth, he first appointed the twelve and then the seventy, he sent them out two by two to prepare the way for his ministry: for the kingdom was at hand. (Matt. 10). After the ascension and Day of Pentecost the Apostles took on greater responsibilities.

While the twelve Apostles seem to have a very special place in God's plan, we read about many other apostles in the Book of Acts. Men are raised up to fill the various ministry needs as the church expands. We need to remember that Jesus is building His church. He listened to the Father in His earthly ministry, and today's believers are also to be led by the Spirit.

Walk in the truth that you know. Jesus is the way, the truth and the life. The Holy Spirit can lead us by a variety of means. As a home church grows too large the Lord will raise up leaders to begin new ones. Our goal should always be to increase in number. One of the biggest challenges and problems is that the church loses its focus on evangelism. This should always remain a central focus for the church. We still love our kids when they grow up and move out. We just don't see them quite as often. Churches that are inward focused only are unhealthy.

We know the first church was scattered from Jerusalem because of persecution. However, it seemed natural for the early Christians to take the message of salvation out to people who had not heard it. Earlier believers who had received the gospel on the Day of Pentecost had returned to their hometowns and taken the gospel with them. Philip had taken the gospel to the Samaritans. Peter preached to Cornelius and his household in Caesarea, and there they were the first Gentiles to receive the Holy Spirit. Many Gentiles began to come into the church. It is amazing that without formal structure the church supernaturally began to spread all over Asia Minor. It was an organic move by the Holy Spirit with no church growth program designed by man.

We read about the great persecutor of the church, Saul, getting converted, and he becomes the great Apostle Paul. It is through his letters to the churches that we can be filled in on more detail of the structure of the early church. While Peter is the great Apostle to the Jews, Paul is sent by the Holy Spirit to preach to Jews and Gentiles. Paul has been raised to know Jewish laws and traditions. Because of his knowledge of the Old Testament he discerns what is truly spiritual and what is just tradition. He understood that the Old Testament was fulfilled in Christ. He understood the position of the church, and the supremacy of Christ. It is not definite that Paul wrote the book of Hebrews, but that letter tells us the importance of the spiritual position of Jesus as intercessor for the church.

When we gather, even if it is two or three, it is important to gather together unto Jesus. He must be lifted-up for the Holy Spirit to minister. This is major!!

Our point of unity is our desire to worship Jesus and hear the Word. Real family friendship will come out of that, but Jesus must remain Central to have unity.

## *Who is the Church?*

Foundation: The church is founded upon a relationship with JESUS. You must be born again in order to see the kingdom of God. (John 3:3) We become a part of the local (by local I mean part of the church of the city you live in) church when we are born again and baptized. Baptism is coming into covenant with the Lord. We receive eternal life when we are born again. This comes with repentance and surrender. Our spirit which was dead in trespasses and sin becomes alive because the Spirit of Christ enters us. After the inward spiritual transformation, we outwardly show our decision to live for Christ through burial in the waters of baptism. In the Old Testament a Jew had to be circumcised as a sign of a covenant relationship. (Col. 2:11,12) Today, in the New Covenant, we are baptized in water.

In Antioch the believers were the first to be called Christians. The believers were called Christians because there was an anointing upon them that the unsaved could see. All believers should desire to be in relationship with the Lord in such a way there is an anointing upon us. Our goal is to be transformed through the renewing of our minds to think and act in obedience to the Word of God. (Romans 12:1-3) (Acts 4:13) The word Christ means anointed one.

In the first four books of the New Testament, we read the four gospels which tell the story of Jesus' life, ministry, death and resurrection. Every believer needs to begin their spiritual walk by reading these four books. Jesus' last words were, "But You shall receive power when the Holy Spirit has come upon you; and you shall be witnesses to Me in Jerusalem and in all Judea and Samaria and to the end of the earth." (Acts 1:8). We see that much of Jesus ministry was in homes, and he also ministered in the streets and marketplaces. I would encourage your home group to spend time examining the ministry of Jesus and the early church in your Bible study. Focus on making disciples of Jesus! A disciple is one who one who accepts and assists in spreading the doctrines of another. (Matthew 28:18-20)

Christians who had scattered at the persecution and death of Stephen had taken the gospel to Antioch. When the apostles in Jerusalem heard the gospel had been received, they sent Barnabas to minister there. He in turn called Paul from Tarsus to come and help him. In your gatherings, you will want to bring in other leadership on occasion. It is important to stay connected with the church at large. Be open and discerning to who the Lord brings along.

After Paul and Barnabas had spent a year teaching in Antioch, a prophet came from Jerusalem named Agabus, who told the church that there was a great famine throughout the world. It was decided to send relief to the brethren dwelling in Judea, so the Antioch church sent relief to the elders in Jerusalem by Paul and Barnabas. We read in Acts Chapter 13 that there were other prophets and teachers in the church at Antioch.

At this time Herod killed James a leading elder in the Jerusalem church. Judgment fell on Herod and because he allowed himself to be proclaimed as God.

He was struck dead and eaten by worms.

## *Drama Happens*

In America we live in an atmosphere where we can still worship freely, but in every group, drama will occur on occasion. Satan is still the enemy of the church. Remember God is on the throne, and He will see you through victorious if you trust Him. However, peace should reign in a home meeting. If peace is broken on a continual basis, the problem should be discerned and corrected.

Do not put God in a box, or the moving of the Holy Spirit in a box, remember we are called to represent the Lord on planet earth. Jesus is head of the church. Jesus taught that leaders are to care for the sheep. We do not want to compare ourselves with others or fall into competition. Jesus is who we desire to please, and he will reward us.

## *Natural Gifts*

There are people gifted in administration and helping. Some call these grace gifts, but life consists of order and need, and we need to plug in where our talents are. (I Corinthians 12:28) Delegate responsibilities in the home meeting that come up to those who enjoy doing them and are capable in that area. Be willing to pitch in wherever needed. Sometimes I think real ministry begins when we do the things that are not that much fun. Yes, it is fun to serve Jesus.

In the next chapter we will look at the basic ministry positions God has placed in the church. Be careful not to say people are in positions they are not qualified for or not serving in that Scriptural capacity. I have heard people called Apostle, who never started a church in their life, and who do not have a heart or the knowledge of scripture to correct church problems. It is time to honor biblical structure as much as we understand it, and not shut our eyes just to maintain peace.

We see the early church did life together. They had jobs to provide for their families and yet they desired to fellowship together and like Israel of the Old Testament, they were an example to those around them who were not covenant people. Our lifestyle and our ministry should reflect the culture of the kingdom of God, just like the early church.

## CHAPTER FOUR
# CALLED AND GIFTED LEADERS

*First Apostles*

There were the original twelve apostles that Jesus called during His earthly ministry, along with Matthias who replaced Judas before Pentecost. We know they are special because in New Jerusalem, the heavenly city, they will have their names written on the twelve foundation stones. These men walked with Jesus when He was on earth. That is special! However, in Acts we see Paul and Barnabas are apostles.

An apostle is someone who starts new churches and corrects problems in the local church. They can appoint elders in the new churches. (Titus 1:5) Apostles are sent out from their home church.

Today, many missionaries operate in that paradigm if they go to an unreached area. We know there are unreached areas in our nation, too.

As we see the church grow and expand there will be apostles raised up. It is noted that apostles in the New Testament were marked by supernatural signs and wonders. (II Corinthians 12:12) These men should know they are called by the Holy Spirit.

*Elders*

Elders in a church have the authority over the local church. In fact, apostles can be received or rejected by the elders. Elders do not have to accept what an apostle tells them. (III John 9) Can you imagine rejecting John the Beloved? It is ultimately the elders place to make decisions for the safety of the local church. Elders should be able to rule and teach. Requirements for elders are listed in I Timothy 2. They can also be called, Bishops.

The Greek word for pastor is also interchangeable with elder. An elder must be blameless, the husband of one wife, temperate, sober-minded, of good behavior, hospitable, able to teach, not given to wine, not violent, not greedy for money, but gentle, not quarrelsome, not covetous; one who rules his own house well, having his children in submission with all reverence. For if a man does not know how to rule his own house, how will he take care of the church of God? He is not to be a novice, lest being puffed up with pride he falls into the same condemnation as the devil. He must have a good testimony among those who are outside, lest he fall into reproach and the snare of the devil.

Let leadership evolve and be recognized. A presbytery is a body of elders and leaders in a church. I Timothy 4:14) In the beginning you may consult with Christian leaders outside your group who are reputable and know your people to confirm your decisions. Consult men and women who love and care about you. The word presbytery is only mentioned once in the Bible. Another illustration would be the calling out of Paul and Barnabas in the Antioch church to be missionaries. They should be leaders who hear from the Holy Spirit and understand what the Lord is doing in the body.

From scripture the elders can have multiple functions. They may be pastors, teachers, prophets, evangelists, or even an apostle. Peter was an apostle, but historically believed to have been a bishop (elder) at Rome. We can see why it is a safety net to have multiple elders with the wisdom of more than just one person. One elder may be more of a natural leader, but the authority is spread out among all the elders. Real spiritual leaders will appreciate this and submit to one another. The safety comes in seeking the head of the church, JESUS, when doing kingdom business. It is easy to get stuck in a traditional mindset when looking at these positions. Paul appointed elders in every church. He did not appoint a pastor to lead the church. It is no wonder we are losing pastors so fast. Leaders may rise to the top, but an authentic servant leader will appreciate sharing the leadership, and he will know how to.

*Deacons*

The deacons took care of distributing goods to the widows and other temporal needs of the church. We read in Acts 6 that in Jerusalem, the first apostles appointed deacons to take care of the temporal needs, so they had time to minister the Word and pray. However, the deacons in the early church also were used in a preaching ministry. We see Philip, a deacon in the church of Jerusalem, preaching in Samaria. Because deacons are in a position of relating to all the church it is important that they are chosen for their heart and their character. (I Timothy 3:8) "Also, deacons must be reverent, not double-tongued, not given to much wine, not greedy for money, holding the mystery of the faith with a pure conscience. Let them also first be proved, then let them who serve as deacons being found blameless. Also, their wives must be reverent, not slanderers, temperate, faithful in all things. Let deacons be the husbands of one wife, ruling their children and their own house well. For those who have served well as deacons obtain for themselves a good standing and great boldness in the faith which is in Christ Jesus."

You may not see the need for deacons in a house church, but there are a lot of hands-on needs in the body of Christ and in the community. Deacons can reach out beyond your group. Temporal ministry is helping widows and orphans. The poor is always with us. Christians are to affect their cities by their lifestyle and their desire to manifest the kingdom of God everywhere they go! (Isaiah 61:4) Remember these giftings can overlap. The Holy Spirit is creative, be open to new ways of spreading the good news.

### *Evangelists*

Philip is known as an evangelist while serving as a deacon. When he led people to the Lord in Samaria, he called the Apostles from Jerusalem to come and pray for the new believers to receive the Holy Spirit. Here we see the ministry offices working together. Our focus should be more on getting the ministry and work done than on putting ourselves in pigeon-holes by labels.

An evangelist today often is known as one who travels full time, but an evangelist is different from an apostle in that an evangelist may work out of a local body and can have responsibilities there. Timothy is encouraged by Paul to do the work of an evangelist. Evangelists should be encouraged and recognized, as should all spiritual endowments in the local church.

Evangelists will inspire others to be soul-winners. Every believer should be able to win people to the Lord and have that desire. (Matthew 28:18-20) Jesus came to seek and save the lost, we are to fulfill the present-day ministry of Jesus.

### *Teachers*

Teachers are mentioned more than any other gift. Elders are to be able to teach. Paul suggested that all believers should grow up in their ability to eventually teach, and not remain babes in the word. There are people gifted in teaching and have an anointing to do so. The church needs teachers who see spiritual truths and have a heart to develop other people's ministries. The real goal of the five-fold ministry listed in Ephesians 4 is to equip the saints for ministry. If a person is self-seeking, they are not going to be able to focus on their student's development in the Lord.

### *Prophets*

Prophets have been since the beginning of time. (Luke 2:70) The charismatic modern church has often seen the office of prophet as something only a few people in the nation are called to. We read in I Corinthians 14 prophets have major ministry in the local church. There should be several prophets that share on a subject when the church gathers together, and then the believers are to discern what the Holy Spirit is saying. Revelation 19:10 tells us that prophecy is the testimony of Jesus. So, we need to hear what He is saying to the church through the prophets. It is a "now' word, where teaching is a general word. A prophet should know what is going on in the spiritual world, the natural world, the local church, and just in general what is the Lord saying to the church. We need to be inspired, corrected, and challenged by a now fresh word when we come together, and the prophets are the men and women who God has anointed to bring His message, along with the other ministry gifts.

The Old Testament prophets were patriots. I believe that the more informed about world events a Christian knows and can discern from a Christian worldview the more effectual they can be in empowering the church. All spiritual gifts grow with use. (Romans 12:6)

### *Pastors*

This is a hard one, because today we see pastors as the ruling elder who often has the full responsibility of ministry on his shoulders, and depending on the church, he may make all the final decisions by himself. The Greek word meaning shepherd is used to describe this office and it is interchanged with the elders of the church. All elders should have a shepherd heart. Jesus is the great Shepherd, and he cares for the sheep. Elders need to remember they are under-shepherds called to care for the Lord's people. Jesus exhorted Peter to feed the sheep. In order to have a healthy church, you must abide in Jesus and allow his word to abide in you. The Christian leader should continue to study and be led by the Holy Spirit.

### *Other ministry listings*

Above are what the church calls the five-fold ministries as listed in Ephesians 4, but in I Corinthians 12:28 through 31 we see some other gifts listed. These seem to be more than just being used in a church service, but in the total life of the church. Their calling is to develop the saints for the work of the ministry. Today's paradigm too often centers on a stage performance by one leader week in and week out. We can see how different this is from what we read in the Book of Acts and the Epistles.

### *Workers of Miracles*

There could be people who have a calling like Elisha and Elijah who seem to be used in miracles more than the average Christian. We know apostles are to be used in miracles. Again, we do not want to compartmentalize the Holy Spirit. God distributes as he sees fit. Every believer should see miracles on occasion or why do we pray to a God with whom nothing is impossible? The gift of miracles seems to go beyond the calling of the average believer.

Jesus works with us confirming the word preached. (Mark 16:20, Matt. 28:20) The more we teach on the power of God, his healing promises, the baptism in the Holy Spirit and the gifts, the more we will see the miracles. If we do not preach the word and teach the word, Jesus has nothing to confirm.

### *Gifts of Healing*

Men like Benny Hinn, Oral Roberts, and women like Kathryn Kuhlman operated as a gift of healing. They are people place in the body with a ministry of healing. They are a gift to the body of Christ.

Remember the word says he will increase our ministry as we step out. "Take heed what you hear. With the same measure you use, it will be measured to you, and to you who hear, more will be given. For whoever has, to him more will be given, but whoever does not have even what he has will be taken away from him." (Mark 4:24,25) The Lord has invested talents in all of us, and as we use those talents for the Lord, he will increase our ministry. It is not surprising that the Holy Spirit would move upon Oral Roberts with the gift of healing, because he taught healing and the Lord confirmed the word. We see people in our midst with the ministry of healing, not just big-name ministers. I know names you would not recognize that have this calling.

### *Gifts of Help and Administrations*

The deacons certainly fall into this category. Many women served Jesus and traveled with him meeting the needs of those who were with him, also. Where there is a need, the Lord will empower someone to fill it. Certain people are especially gifted in administrations. God is interested in the details of our lives and the life of the church. Everything we do should be to bring glory to the Lord.

The Lord spoke to me that we would minister to the poor, and he gave my husband and I the ability to organize a ministry to the homeless in his hometown. I have put together three beginning women's shelters in different cities. The ability to organize and plan has equipped us for the gift of administrations. We attended conferences, visited other missions and street ministries, but in hindsight I can see it has been the leading of the Lord and the Holy Spirit. In the natural as a small-town girl, with no experience of a culture outside of a farm town, homeless shelters is not a natural calling. We have been in a variety of ministry situations where this gift has been needed. I am a big picture person and have seen the need for teamwork and that it is only as we work as the body of Christ that the kingdom can advance.

## *Variety of Tongues*

The early Pentecostals from the 1900's Azusa Street revival took off to foreign mission fields trusting the Lord to supernaturally give them the language. There is faith and there is presumption! We need to seek the Lord for the best gifts! (Corinthians 12:31) The tongues listed in I Corinthians 12:30, are supernatural tongues, but as listed in I Corinthians 12:26, it could be learned languages, which would be a definite gift when ministering multi-culturally or it could be talking about spiritual tongues.

# CHAPTER FIVE
# NINE GIFTS OF THE SPIRIT

*Some Background*

I believe what I am going to share is very clear and obvious, but when we have only experienced a certain form of worship or church service, it is hard to visualize what the Bible says, or accept it is for this time in history. Remember, tradition can void the power of God. I come to my conclusions from studying great Pentecostal revivals of the past, the charismatic renewal I am a part of and most importantly from the writings of the apostles and the Book of Acts in the New Testament.

The first century church met for worship as a gathering of people whose spiritual life did not fit into the previous form of worship. That was also true of our experience in the charismatic move in the seventies when God moved through home meetings that were held outside the organized church. People gathered together in homes who attended Lutheran, Methodist, Catholic and Baptist churches but who had received the Baptism in the Holy Spirit and tasted of the power of Pentecost.

The home meetings we attended were not called house churches. We all went to traditional churches, and we just met from house to house on the side. Before I get into how those meetings were conducted, I am going to go over the gifts of the Holy Spirit, because much of what we learned has been lost to many in this new generation land those who have only attended traditional Pentecostal churches.

Many pastors did not like the fact that these home meetings were inter denominational or "not under a specific covering, pastor or denomination." It is true that some pretty weird teaching came through that movement, but the Bible teaches us that there were false teachers and false doctrine that tried to corrupt the first century church, too. That is why Paul wrote the epistles to the churches. God is faithful to protect those who love the truth. (II Thess. 2:10) The early church met in homes, and the meetings we saw spring up across the nation in homes was an organic move of the Holy Spirit.

Paul likens the church as the 'body' of Christ in Ephesians. In I Corinthians 12:14. Paul writes that the body is not one member but many. In fact, in I Cor. 12:12 and 13 he says we are all baptized into the body of Christ. He says in verse 13, and in Galatians 3:26-29 the body of Christ is not to be divided by race, social standing or whether we are male or female, but we are all heirs according to promise. Everyone is on level playing field when it comes to being a functioning part of the body of Christ. The Apostle Paul said that we are to count each part (person) as an important part of the body. (Not just a pew sitter.)

*Jesus' Ministry is our Example*

I want to insert here, that Jesus' life and ministry was not separated into spiritual and secular. Neither was the life of the early church. The sons of God are those who LIVE according to the Spirit and not after the flesh. Our minds are to be set on the things of the

Spirit. (Romans 8) As Christ-followers our relationship with Jesus affects how we keep house, raise children, work at our vocations, vote, etc. Jesus commandment was that we love HIM with all our heart, soul, mind and strength. That encompasses the "life" of the believer and should be a demonstration of how the church does "life" together. We are ambassadors for the kingdom of God while on earth, and we should represent the kingdom as individuals and corporately by our lifestyle. His kingdom is a kingdom of righteousness. (Matthew 7:23) Believers are also considered the 'family' of God.

Being a participating disciple in spiritual ministry was a mark of the Charismatic Renewal, which was also sometimes called the "Jesus movement," that we were a part of. Everyone wanted to be used in ministry, and it was in the home meetings that most of us learned to operate in the gifts of the Spirit. It is much easier to respond in faith to the anointing of the Spirit in a group of fifteen than it is in a large church gathering.

When we gather to meet for worship, we should all to be open to be used by the gifts of the Spirit. Also, outside of the church gathering, as we live our lives, we should be open to the Holy Spirit moving through us. The great awakenings of the past have been as individuals passionately lived for Jesus, and they changed our nation. We read this in the book of Acts as they reached the then known world in a few short years.

Also, today there is no excuse for limiting your growth to a certain denomination's traditions. If your walk in the Lord is fear based, you need to get into the word for yourself and trust the Lord to give you discernment. The Bible says that God has given us each a teacher to reside in us who is called the Holy Spirit. (I John 2:27) This does not mean that we don't grow in revelation knowledge and receive teaching from other anointed people. (Matt. 23:9-12) None of us know all there is to know about the kingdom of God. That is part of the joy of knowing Jesus.

Healings, miracles and radically changed lives were a part of the Charismatic Renewal, but too often today the gifts have been relegated out of many church services. The gifts of the Spirit are operated by faith, not our minds and intellect only.

### *Gifts Operate in an Atmosphere*

The gifts move in an atmosphere. What is that atmosphere? It is when people come together because they love Jesus and expect to see the Holy Spirit move through the gifts. Yes, we wanted to learn as new believers, but we primarily came together out of a love relationship with the Lord. We expected and desired for the Holy Spirit to use us, and we came hungry to hear the Word! We must welcome the Holy Spirit in our midst if we want an atmosphere for him to move.

Bill Johnson of Bethel Church in Redding California wrote a book, <u>Hosting the Presence</u>. It is worth reading. In fact, this may be a good place to encourage you that part of growing and keeping your first love is not only reading your Bible but reading good books by anointed leaders.

However, too often in the past and today we see Christians looking to leaders who are on television or written up in magazines and do not recognize who the Lord desires to use in their own midst. We will never see revival that really changes a city when we do not accept the anointed ministry that the Lord places among us. The Bible teaches us to receive who the Lord sends our way, and we will receive the same reward. (Matt. 10:41) We are part of a local body of believers in God's plan for a given area. Remember Jesus said a prophet is without honor in his own hometown. The Jews couldn't receive a Messiah that came from Nazareth, and even Jesus could not do many mighty works there. If we want in on the move of God, we need to accept the giftings in one another. Jesus is Lord of the Harvest!

It is the ministries in the local church that you want to see develop. God has placed the body together as he sees fit. All teaching must agree with the Bible, the final authority. Too many traditional churches do not train people to be leaders. I believe in a strong church any leader can leave, and the church should be able to continue.

The goal of a home church or meeting should be to grow in the Lord and to sharpen and encourage one another. People have issues come up that need personal prayer, etc., but do not fall into the pattern of ministering at the lowest common denominator. Remember the Lord responds to faith. Stay positive and preach a redemptive, victorious word. We are changed through the renewing of the mind by the word, not counseling. Correction and truth are not opposed to compassion. Keep first things first! Let the strong speak, and the weak be encouraged.

Remember that it is in an atmosphere of worship that the Holy Spirit moves, and one touch from the Holy Spirit, or one prophecy can often do more than many words sometimes. The Holy Spirit is our helper, our comforter, our "Jesus in the Now!" Be a church family who supports and shows compassion that helps meet real need, but do not let problems monopolize your church service.

There is a place for Christian counseling, but the church today has begun to lean on the arm of flesh rather than the Holy Spirit who was sent to change us. We can encourage and teach spiritual truth, but it is the Holy Spirit that does the work of transforming and truly setting free!

### *Different Administrations*

The gifts of the Spirit are listed in I Corinthians 12:4-10. We need to read I Corinthians 12:1-14 to see that while these gifts may operate differently through different individuals or have different administrations, it is the same Lord who is inspiring them. The Holy Spirit will move on people, and they will respond by faith. Since we all have difference personalities the gifts will have diversity as we respond to the Holy Spirit. In other words, some prophecy may not come forth in perfect grammar. Some people may be loud, others quiet. Etc.

### *The Church's Authority*

We cannot divide the trinity. God the Father is Spirit. Jesus was God in the flesh. He showed us kingdom living and ministry during his time on earth. The Holy Spirit has been sent back to reveal Jesus and the kingdom of God to the world and to minister to the church. Jesus commissioned us to win the world to himself through the word preached and signs and wonders. The Holy Spirit is God in the NOW, and he reveals Jesus' present-day-ministry through us in the church and in the world. Jesus ministered by being obedient to what the Father showed him, and the Holy Spirit did the work. We abide in Jesus and allow his words to abide in us. We live in a spiritual realm where the supernatural should become natural.

Another way of saying this is God has a plan for the ages. It began in Genesis. The Jews were his special people. From that lineage Jesus was born, even though He was born of the Holy Spirit, there was a natural lineage also. The cross was a part of that plan. Jesus defeated the devil and elevated New Testament believers to receive back what Adam lost at the fall. Now as believers we are to carry on his ministry until Jesus returns, and that plan means we stay connected to the Godhead in the same way Jesus did when he walked the earth.

### *Operation of the Gifts*

The gifts are given to profit the church through edification, teaching, exhortation and guidance.

While some people operate in one gift more than another, we do not own these gifts. There are different opinions on this, but God is sovereign, and many people are anointed in several of these gifts. However, it seems people have faith, or it is God's choice to use them in certain ones more predominately. However, Jesus is our example, and we will be anointed to be used in the gifts as the need arises as we minister in Jesus name. We should all be open to being obedient to whatever gift the Holy Spirit desires to use through us. We are told to minister according to our faith, so we can expect to see more ministry like in the Book of

Acts as we respond to the anointing.

*The Nine Gifts listed in I Corinthians*

There are nine gifts listed in I Corinthians 12, and we will divide them into three groups.

*Revelation or Knowing Gifts:*
*Knowledge, Wisdom, and Discerning of Spirit*

The first group is revelation or 'knowing' gifts. The Word of Knowledge is the manifestation of a truth that you did not study or determine ahead of time. You just know the Holy Spirit has given you a wise bit of knowledge in an instant for a certain need or situation.

The next gift we will look at is a Word of Wisdom. This shows us what to do or say in a certain situation by the leading of the Holy Spirit. It is instantly dropped in our minds by the Spirit, and it is not wisdom we have learned. There is Godly wisdom and knowledge that comes with study and walking with the Lord. Christian growth is part of discipleship. However, the Word of Wisdom and the Word of Knowledge are instant and not learned but are given through the Holy Spirit.

The third knowing gift is Discernment of Spirits. Teaching on deliverance is important, because one fourth of Jesus ministry was delivering people from demons. As our nation gets more sinful, there is more need for deliverance. Sin gives a platform in people's lives to the devil. However, we do not want to go beyond what the word teaches on this subject because witchcraft is a lust of the flesh, and deliverance is one of the most abused areas if it is taken out of scriptural context. Simply put, Jesus took away the power of Satan and defeated him on the cross. In Mark 16:17

Jesus gave us the authority to cast out devils in his name. Keep is simple, knowing all authority in heaven and earth is behind the name of Jesus. If a person desires deliverance, they will be delivered! Do not become a Pharisee in this area and think you can come up with formulas beyond what is in the scripture.

All glory is in JESUS defeating Satan. (I John 3:8) I do not read where Jesus took hours delivering people. He exhorted his disciples to fast and pray when they could not deliver a demoniac. In other words, make sure you are right with the Lord. The disciples had been debating who was the greatest, which may have been their problem when they ran into a young person that wasn't delivered. (Mark 9:33) I have seen people give the devil too much attention by teaching on deliverance as a platform for their ministry. Whenever a minister's technique gets the glory instead of Jesus, there is an ego problem. Corrie Ten Boon, a saint who hid Jews during WW 2, said, "Look without be distressed, look within be depressed, look to Jesus be at rest." When deliverance is naval gazing at all the areas of sin and brokenness in mankind, and all the lusts of the flesh, we dilute the authority and power Jesus gave us in the name of JESUS. We are changed from glory to glory as we gaze upon Jesus and renew our minds in the word. Do not let your home meeting turn into deliverance sessions, even though deliverance may take place as the Lord leads.

In Acts 16:16 Paul did not immediately discern the problem of the young girl following them or he just took his time to deliver the lady, but he gave a simple command and set her free. Casting the demon out of the slave girl landed them in prison so that may be why he took his time in casting the devil out of her. Paul walked in holiness and he knew the authority Jesus had given him. The Gift of Discernment is not limited to demons. You also can discern flesh from Spirit. We learn discernment with use, (Hebrews 5:14) but the Gift of Discernment is an instant knowledge dropped into us by the Holy Spirit. It is a manifestation at a given time for a certain situation.

Maybe this is a good time to remind us that the word says if we need wisdom, we should ask for it. The Holy Spirit is omnipresent. Jesus said he will never leave us or forsake us. Christian ministry is man and God working together. There is a word I like to use: synergy. In the American Heritage Dictionary, they use the example that the doctrine of regeneration is affected by a combination of human will and divine grace. In other words, man repents and turns to the Lord with his whole heart, and God puts his Spirit within him and makes him a new creation. Man has his part in the process. Expect God to anoint you! Faith is knowing what God wills and acting on it. We will be judged by our obedience in responding to the Holy Spirit at the Judgment Seat of Christ. (I Corinthians 3:13-15, Colossians 3:17,23,24)

When it comes to discernment, we must always remember that the Bible is our absolute authority. The Bible is Spirit and Truth. (John 17:17) We will be judged by the word of God when we stand before Him. Anything said or done that does not line up with the Word is flesh or false teaching. The spiritual man judges all things. (I Corinthians 2:15) The root word in this situation means to "see through." The church needs discernment with mercy!

## *The Utterance Gifts:*
*Tongues, Interpretation, and Prophecy*

The second group of gifts of the Holy Spirit mentioned in I Corinthians 12 are called the utterance gifts, or the speaking gifts. They are the Gift of Tongues, Interpretation of Tongues and Prophecy.

In I Corinthians 12:30 Paul said, "Do all speak in tongues?" Here he is saying a special anointing will come upon a believer to give a message in tongues. This is not an "at will" message, but like the other nine gifts listed in I Corinthians 12 is a message inspired by the Holy Spirit for that moment given by a believer who is prompted by the Holy Spirit to speak the tongues forth. This is mentioned in I Corinthians 14:27 where Paul says, "Let two or three at the most give a message in tongues and let one interpret, but if there is no interpreter, let him keep silent in church and let him speak to himself and to God." Notice the last part of that sentence says tongues that are not interpreted is speaking to yourself and God. There are two kinds of tongues. One is given at the baptism in the Holy Spirit, as in Acts 2 and at Cornelius house in Acts 10:45. Every believer can pray in tongues or pray in the spirit. (I Corinthians 14:14.15.18) This is done at the will of the believer, with no special unction during their private prayer time, and it is appropriate in a Pentecostal prayer meeting or time when prayer is appropriate.

However, the "Gift of Tongues" is only to be used when the Holy Spirit prompts a message. This will always be followed with an interpretation. After a message in tongues is given, the Holy Spirit prompts a person to speak forth an interpretation in the language people understand. If you are prompted to give a message in tongues, you can rest assured the Holy Spirit will anoint you or someone else to give the interpretation. The message is not a translation, it is an interpretation. They may not be the same length, etc. There are a variety of tongues. In other words, they may not all sound alike. The gift of tongues and the gift of interpretation go together, and they are equal to the gift of prophecy. They are prompted by the Holy Spirit at an appropriate time. When Paul says an interpreter must be there, I believe he is saying tongues must be the Gift of Tongues and don't just be praying in tongues. (I Corinthians 14:28)

My opinion, from I Corinthians 14:22, is that the reason the Holy Spirit moves through tongues and interpretation instead of just the Gift of Prophecy is that unbelievers notice that something supernatural is being said. The Gift of Prophecy is when the Holy Spirit moves on a believer to speak out a word for the body that is at that instant dropped into their spirit. You will feel an unction to speak it, and there is always an element of faith needed. I have heard some say that the Gift of tongues is used for a foreigner to hear and know the language that is given in tongues. This has happened but it is not the norm.

In the Book of Revelation, it says the spirit of prophecy is the testimony of Jesus. (Rev. 19:10) These utterance gifts are Jesus speaking to the believers now by means of the Holy Spirit. It is a fresh word from heaven. Jesus is still the Head of the body, or the church, and he desires to speak to his people, through his people. No wonder Paul exhorts us to desire to prophecy, and to covet the gift!

God is a God of order. The Bible tells us that we have control of our own spirit. As we move in the gifts of the Spirit we will not interrupt when someone else is speaking, etc. In a home meeting it is easy to know when the Holy Spirit is moving and when to speak out, or to operate in these gifts. In larger meetings you need to follow the custom of the place you are at. This has limited this generation from learning to experience how to move in the gifts. You may break custom if you are sure it is the leading of the Lord! Jesus worked outside the customs of the religious traditions of his day but use discernment.

While the Word outlines these truths, it is still important to know that God is sovereign. I remember a time when my next-door neighbor who was chairman of a large Christian Women's Club was part of a denomination that did not accept the gifts for today. However, she was a strong born-again disciple and a soul-winning Christian. She attended a home meeting with me and when a Gift of tongues was given, she gave the interpretation. The Holy Spirit used her, even though she had not yet been Baptized in the Holy Spirit and received her prayer language. (She did later.)

I would encourage you to treat the things of God with reverence. I have heard people prophecy out of their own spirit. Do not say, "Thus says the Lord", when he hasn't. Instead just pray for the situation or person, and if it is anointed, they will receive from the Lord. I have seen some people give a prophetic exhortation and call it the "gift of prophecy", but it is a different operation than the Gift of Prophecy that is instantaneous like tongues and interpretation.

I have been used in the Gift of Prophecy, and I do

not know what I am going to say beyond the first few words. Many have the same experience when giving a word of prophecy. In a large group it is a blessing to have an interpretation of tongues instead of prophecy. This has happened to me several times, and in my opinion, it gives more credibility by getting the people's attention that something supernatural is happening. I have also been used in prophetic exhortation, and only speak it when I know it is the leading of the Holy Spirit and it is appropriate for the setting. An exhortation is like a short word, that is burning in your heart, and you know the Lord wants you to share it with the group. We rejoice that God is speaking through his people!

Again, there are diversities of workings the Bible says, so I do not want to limit the Holy Spirit into my limited experience. Some people see pictures. I do not see this listed in the gifts in the New Testament, but Peter had a vision of a sheet let down with unclean animals. God spoke to a couple of prophets in the Old Testament this way, but they knew what the Lord was saying to them. If you believe the Holy Spirit is showing you something in the Spirit pray for the interpretation. Do not bring confusion by not having a clear revelation or teaching.

*Power Gifts:*
*Healing, Faith, and Miracles*

The last set of three gifts listed in I Corinthians 12 are the Power gifts. When Jesus left the earth, he gave the Holy Spirit to the church to reveal his power and authority over the devil, and to manifest the kingdom of God. The Power gifts are a continuance of the ministry that Jesus had when he walked the earth. He exhorted his followers to do the works that he did, and that they were to do even greater works. The gifts operate in an atmosphere of love, faith and compassion. God desires for us to believe him and move in supernatural ways! Read the book of Acts!!

When Jesus ascended and sent back the Holy Spirit, he gave commandment to go minister in his name. We have legal authority when we are born again into the family of God. It is our inherited position to have authority just like Jesus did when he walked the earth. In fact, the Word says that He confirms the Word we preach until the end of the age. (Mark 16:20) How does Jesus do that? By the Spirit!

Let's remember here, that we do not earn these gifts. They are operated in response to the Holy Spirit's leading. In fact, in Matt. 7:23 It says people who operate in these gifts and practice lawlessness will be rejected by Jesus when he returns. The Holy Spirit spoke through a donkey in Balaam's day, so we should never feel proud when God uses us in the gifts. It is a humbling thing to have the Lord use us, but we always need to remember that without holiness, no man shall see the Lord. We are ambassadors for the kingdom, children of God. We want to live lives that bring glory to the Lord.

The three power gifts are the Gift of Faith, the Gift of Miracles and the Gift of Healing. The Gift of Faith is the first power gift we will look at. It is a supernatural faith that comes into a believer at a certain time to meet a certain need! Act on it! It still takes responding to the unction of the Holy Spirit. This gift is usually in operation with the Gift of Healing or Miracles. Healing can come through the Gift of Faith, but the Gift of Faith can come upon a brand-new believer or whosoever the Lord chooses. It is the Lord moving through a person for that moment for that situation!

There is a faith in God that grows with studying the word, walking with the Lord in obedience and experiencing answers to prayer. Again, I want to remind you that the Lord is omnipresent, and you can pray for healing any time because God promises it in his Word. Remember Jesus couldn't do many miracles in his hometown because of unbelief. (Mark 6:4)

Oral Roberts and other healing evangelists had healing ministries. They had developed faith in the area of healing, and they had healing ministries. They taught a clear healing message from the Word of God, and the Lord confirmed their message. However, the Gift of healing would come upon him at certain times, and Oral said, he knew everyone would be healed during that time of God's special presence. He combined his healing ministry as in I Cor. 12:28 and the Gift of healing as in I Corinthians 12:9 was working through him on occasion.

Do all have gifts of healing? No, we are not all called to have a ministry like a healing evangelist, but we can all be used by the Holy Spirit in praying for the sick. The Gift of Healing is the Holy Spirit moving sovereignly through a believer to do a work beyond that person's normal faith level.

I would encourage you to pray in faith when people desire prayer because the word tells us to pray for the sick and preach the gospel to all people. We do not have to wait for a special anointing to be obedient to the word, but we do need to use wisdom and discernment on when and where. In many home gatherings we have a 'hot seat' at the end of the meeting where we pray over people with needs, and often it is a healing need. During these times there seems to be a special anointing for the Holy Spirit to speak and move through the gifts.

In I Corinthians 12:4-6, it mentions diversity of gifts, ministries and activities, but it is the same God who works all in all. In verse seven the manifestation of the Spirit is given to each one for the profit of all. In an environment when the Holy Spirit is moving, some have felt heat in their hands and knew it was the Lord desiring to use them for healing. Others feel a sensation in a certain area of their body, and it is a combination of the word of knowledge and healing, and they speak out that God is desiring to heal in that area. We do not want to put how God moves in a box but learn to be led by the Spirit. Healing cans be instantaneous or like the ten lepers. They were healed as they went. Salvation and healing have already been purchased and paid for at the cross, and we receive by faith.

Miracles are manifestations such as when the four thousand were fed with a few loaves and fishes in Jesus ministry. Many people have experienced miracles of provision, and God desires to do miracles. Stephen, full of faith and power, did great wonders and signs among the people. (Acts 6:8) Philip ministered to multitudes and when they heard the things spoken by him, hearing and seeing the miracles which he did, a great revival took place. Unclean spirits came out of people and healings took place. (Acts8:6)

What are miracles? They are the things that Jesus

did when he ministered, and we are commissioned to expect the same. The Holy Spirit will lead us into these manifestations of the Spirit. Faith is believing the Word is true and acting on it.

We are not to be negative about large television ministries or para-church ministries or churches, just because we see the wisdom and need for small groups to have authentic New Testament church services. Our diverse God will judge all things in the end, and all these people are His servants. God's kingdom is shaped by the head of the church and his name is JESUS!! He has a larger vision and picture of the kingdom than we can imagine, and it takes diversity to spread that kingdom to all nations and people groups.

The Pharisees did not receive Jesus as their Messiah because his ministry was different from the religious system of the day. We want to abide in Him and let his word abide in us. He promises to direct our plans and even our thoughts as we commit our work to him. We know Jesus is returning for a church that has faith and is eagerly waiting for His return. Like the ten wise virgins in Matt. 25, we just need to stay full of the oil of the Holy Spirit.

We do not want to be rigid in the things of the Spirit. God answers prayer, and we are expected to pray in faith believing. How does God answer prayer? He answers by supernatural means. The Holy Spirit is involved, and angels are often involved. (Matthew 4:6) (Ps. 91:11) We need to appreciate the spiritual world that we live in! He gives his angels charge over us to keep us in all our ways.

When it comes to angels, I do not see humans, or

Jesus during his earthly ministry commanding angels to do things. They respond to the Word. The only spiritual beings we are to be instructed to deal with is resisting the devil and casting out demons.

However, we may entertain angels unaware the Bible tells us. God sent an angel to speak to Mary about the incarnation. An angel spoke to Daniel. Angels can manifest in God's sovereign plan to do a specific job, but my caution would be leave angels for God to disperse. I believe we are all protected by angels a lot more than we realize. The Bible says every child has a special angel before the throne of God. (Matthew 18:10) I know each of us have angels watching over us. However, our communication is with the Father in Jesus name. We are to glorify Jesus, not angels. Gnosticism is a problem that Paul wrote to the Colossians about. It is 'spirituality' that is outside the Word of God that is nebulous and leads to spiritual pride.

## CHAPTER SIX
## HAVING CHURCH IN A NEW TESTAMENT MANNER

The first century church automatically moved in the Holy Spirit when they gathered. It is not all about structure, because there are no hard and fast rules in the Word on exactly how they had a service, but we can clearly see the heart of how they met in the first century. The Christians left temple worship when Jerusalem was over run and the temple was destroyed in 70 AD. Then the apostles went forth and preached in the synagogues, but persecution pushed out the true believers even from the synagogues. Judaism and Christianity did not mix.

In Matthew six, Jesus last ministry with the disciples was serving them what we call communion and then they sang a hymn before they went out to the Mount of Olives. I believe ministry can flow in a variety, but natural way when we come together.

First, we will look at how the church seems to operate today. Recently I re-read a book on Charismatic Gifts by a leader who was a part of the healing revival of the 1950's. His bible school continues to this day. It had been years since I had read it and I was surprised at his strict traditional view of the role of pastor. This was written before the mega churches came into existence, and most churches comprised of one pastor and maybe a young pastor. He said if the pastor did not fulfill all the duties he outlined in his book, someone else was liable take his place. I felt the pressure on a pastor just reading about it. Included was hospital and shut in visitation, three fresh sermons a week, two hours of prayer and study daily, reading Christian books, community involvement, be the church administrator and a myriad of other virtues and expectations. No wonder pastors are dropping like flies if they are under that type of pressure, especially the fear someone might replace any of his duties.

Today, in the new church growth paradigms, the mega churches must be run like businesses because of their huge budgets. The responsibilities of the running of the church is delegated more through associate pastors and office personnel. The church is multi-faceted in the services they offer. However, the stage is still the focus for most church attendees, and people expect to get blessed by the performance.

Although opportunities for relationships in small groups may be offered at a mega church, a small percentage of Sunday attendees take advantage of them. Many attend churches twice a month and consider that enough Christian involvement in the church. Many believers are not attending church at all.

Statistics tell us most church growth is people transferring from different churches, not new converts. This is because sheep beget sheep, and when people are not personally involved, they have less tendency to be concerned about bringing others. They are doing good to get to church themselves. I know in the U.S. Assemblies of God only three in ten churches are growing and seventy percent are either plateaued or declining. The Assemblies fares better than many denominations.

Many charismatic leaders are encouraging the 'seven mountains' movement knowing that the church should be affecting every area of society. (education, business, government, family, church, entertainment and the arts) Yes, people are called to vocations by the Holy Spirit. Taking Christian values into the world sounds good and it is good, but a vocation doesn't fulfill the hunger to be used by the Holy Spirit and be a spiritual part of the church. The life of the Christian should affect all areas of their lives, but this is not the ministry of the New Testament believer as outlined in the Bible. Even the Apostle Paul made tents to support himself when the need was there. Do not keep God in a box of traditions that is not scriptural!

How many people groan when the pastor says your ministry is to be an usher! No one is too good to bake cookies and hand out bulletins, but there should be a fire in us to share more than that when we gather together. Doesn't the bible tell us that we can all prophecy one by one?

Christians live life, and the world should observe that we are different. We should care for the widows and the orphans in the church which the Bible tells us is true ministry. In history most social change came from the influence of the church. The churches influence brought prison reform, child labor laws, and many other benefits we appreciate in the American culture. We will give an account when we stand before the judgment seat of Christ for how we lived life and influenced our generation for the Lord.

Many revivals come from young people. I

remember our early days how the young neighborhood kids would pile in with the Lutheran, Catholic and other assorted adults who had gathered in our home. Many young people came from dysfunctional homes and their connection with our family helped them stay in the faith even as they began to attend a church. We all need love and relationships, and the love only God can provide.

Again, our walk with Christ stays fresh when we remember he has called us to tell others how to have eternal life. Always remember people are going to heaven or hell when they die, and we are all going to die unless Jesus comes back in our lifetime. Satan would blind us to this. The false teaching of ultimate reconciliation is growing in our humanistic, tolerant society. It is a teaching that everyone will go to heaven. The Bible talks a lot about hell! We have left repentance out of the prayer for salvation. The New Testament believers preached repentance!

Hebrews 10 says we are to consider one another in order to stir up love and good works, not forsaking the assembling of ourselves together, as is the manner of some, but exhorting one another and so much more as you see the Day approaching. Think about the importance of this! Does the church paradigm allow for exhorting one another?

Prayer, too, is one of the most important ministries of the church. Jesus said his house was to be called a house of prayer. What a privilege to be able to approach the throne of grace in heaven through prayer. All the promises of God find their yes and amen in Christ Jesus! (II Corinthians 1:20) "But we all, with unveiled face, beholding as in a mirror the glory of the

Lord, are being transformed into the same image from glory to glory, just as by the Spirit of the Lord. (II Cor. 3:18) Prayer is about getting into the presence of God. We worship an invisible God, but the Spirit is like the wind. We know He is real! Worship and prayer are how we communicate with God. When we get together to meet with the risen Lord we need to come in an attitude of prayer. Some gatherings should be designated as prayer meetings in seems.

I am not going to address in detail the functions of fellowship, discipleship, evangelism and worship. Like prayer, there are volumes written on each of them. I am going to focus on a New Testament model of having church that I see the Apostle Paul outlines for us. Right attitudes will bring right application as we seek the Lord.

### *Gathering Together unto Jesus!*

When we have "church" we gather together unto Jesus! I Corinthians 14 is an example as the Apostle Paul says, in verse 26, "Whenever you come together." The New Testament church gathers to meet with the risen Christ and with other dedicated believers in the local body of Christ expecting the Holy Spirit to lead the meeting. That is the New Testament model.

In Chapter twelve of I Corinthians we read about the ministry gifts that should flow when we gather together, and we went over them in the last chapter. Arthur Katz, a part of the charismatic renewal said that if everyone who gathers is of the same ethnic and social strata, they are probably meeting in the flesh. I do not know if this is always true, but we do know the scripture tells us that the body of Christ is made up of who-so-ever will follow JESUS.

## *An Exclusive or Arrogant Spirit*

I Corinthians chapter one warns us not to divide from the rest of the body of Christ by saying we follow Paul or Apollos or even by saying "I am of Christ". Many churches have an exclusive spirit. The Galatians had a problem with people who wanted to exclude others that people may be zealous for them, and Paul corrected them! (Galatians 4:17) I guess they were playing hard to get, and somehow religious flesh is attracted to that! (Pharisee spirit) Jesus demands us to recognize that we are a part of the body at large even though we may meet as a home church.

It is natural to think our church or group is the "best or right" one, but we do not really know that is true! We are not all called to marry the same person, and we are not all called to the same church, but believers should never have a proud attitude or a divisive attitude.

I remember leading the first chapter of Aglow in Indianapolis, and the Lord said, do not lift-up "Aglow" but lift-up Jesus. You may attend a traditional church as well as be in a home group, but if you want unity you will not lift-up your church at your home gathering. It will kill the anointing. Jesus is to be who is worshipped. We gather together unto HIM.

You are the temple of the Holy Spirit. If anyone defiles the temple of God, God will destroy him. For the temple of God is holy, whose temple you are. (I Cor. 3:16, 17) That is an awesome thought! The Holy Spirit dwells within each believer. We are to stir up the gifts that are within us. Christ in you, the hope of glory.

You are the body of Christ. The desire of the church should be to present every man perfect in Christ Jesus. This is discipleship. (Col. 1:27-29) We take care of our natural body. If we break a finger, we give that finger a lot of attention until it heals. We should have the same concern for one another. We gather together to build up the body by sharing the word, through psalms, and hymns and spiritual songs, and through the gifts of the Spirit.

When the church comes together it is to teach, encourage, correct, and equip believers for a lifestyle that reflects the life of Christ to the world. From the beginning of time, God has desired a family that represents him well.

It would be so easy to go down rabbit trails, but I want to stick with having a scriptural home meeting. We see that those who are born-again with the Spirit of Christ within them should have a passion to gather together with others to worship, learn, and have the Holy Spirit minister to and through them! If you are going to gather "just" to meet with friends, it is not church. If you are meeting for the worship alone, it is not 'church.' There are times you can do these things.

If your focus of going to a meeting is just to hear the preacher, it is a wrong focus. Today with social media you can hear anointed preaching from preachers anywhere in the world. We come together to be with each other to allow the Holy Spirit to minister in the gifts of the Spirit and to worship Jesus.

In I Corinthians 13, we are exhorted to love one another. This is not sloppy agape! It is not being tolerant of 'stupid.' Oops, my sarcasm is showing! I love the verse in I John 5:2. It tells us that by this we know that we love the children of God, when we love God and keep his commandments. So how do you display love for the brethren? By obeying the commandments! Jesus taught us our righteousness should exceed the ten commandments, (Matt. 5:20) so by living in holiness we are trustworthy, honest, and by the fruit of the Spirit we show forth our love for the brethren. Our Christian love will flow out of who we are, not just what we do. Jesus came to give us power to live the Christian life. (I John 1)

*Discipline*

When it comes to discipline, this is spelled out. I am not going to get into the nitty gritty, but love covers a multitude of sins. Then there is sin that must be dealt with for the salvation of souls and the witness of the church. When it comes to the church, the elders should address sin for the protection of the body. The Holy Spirit should give direction on how to, and there are scriptures to be followed. (Matt. 18:15-20) Remember preaching and teaching the anointed word changes peoples thinking and hearts.

## CHAPTER SEVEN
## A MEETING IN A HOME

Okay, we have all arrived at your house ready and expecting to be blessed! In I Corinthians 14:23 Paul begins by saying this is not a prayer meeting, so do not come and spend all your time praying in tongues. He does not put down speaking in tongues, in fact he says, he prays in tongues more than anyone, but not in a church service when we are going to hear from God. We ae going to have some inter-action with other believers as we focus on the Lord. (I Cor. 14:19)

If unbelievers are present, they recognize the anointing that comes with the believers. Expect the gifts of the Holy Spirit to be activated. The Holy Spirit will speak directly to those unbelievers who are visiting if they come in with a seeking heart! It is interesting to note that Paul said that all can prophesy. In a home meeting the Holy Spirit can move upon every member to give a word of prophesy. This is exciting!

In Verse 26, Paul begins to share about the order of a service. We see inter-action in that each has a psalm, a teaching, a tongue, a revelation, an interpretation. All things are to be done for edification. Col 3:16 "Let the word of Christ dwell in you richly in all wisdom, teaching and admonishing one another in psalms and hymns and spiritual songs, singing with grace in your hearts to the Lord." What we see in theses scriptures is a freedom of participation.

When people come in it is good to greet new

people, and make people feel like you know they are there. Have you ever been to a small group where new people are ignored? Our attitude is to include. We are family! Quickly gather together and get all eyes on the Lord. Worship is so important. We have psalms, hymns and spiritual songs mentioned in Ephesians 5:19. Some people will be anointed to lead in songs. During this time, expect the Holy Spirit to begin to move through the gifts. Take your time to hear a fresh exhortation, a word of knowledge, or whatever and however the Lord desires to move. Good leaders should be spiritual facilitators.

In verse I Cor. 14:29-33 Paul says to let two or three prophets speak and the others weigh what is said. This is talking about the gifted men who are prophets in the church. They will teach on a revelation that they have gotten through study and prayer. The church will discern and enjoy the teaching. They may be talking about the same spiritual subject, maybe not. It does say that we do not have to accept everything, but to discern what we hear. Only Jesus has all perfect knowledge and revelation! We honor men, but we worship JESUS!

Part of the purpose we gather is to grow in our faith. We are disciples striving to be like Jesus. The Bible teaches that we each have the Holy Spirit within us to teach us. (I John 2:27) We are responsible for our own salvation. We should be able to discern truth and grow from the word brought forth through the prophets, teachers and evangelists. Each church service could be different. The elders are to make sure the church is healthy.

Often planning is needed for different types of

meetings. A special occasion or speaker, or a special topic may be needed to be addressed. Just be open to the Lord having his way. God is a God of order and expects us to use wisdom!

# CHAPTER EIGHT
# WOMEN IN THE CHURCH

What about women? I believe many do not like to teach on I Cor. 14 because Paul goes on to say women are to keep silent in the church. This is a little awkward to accept at first glance when today's church is made up of more women than men. I believe Paul is bringing correction to the Corinthian church. Perhaps, they were following Jewish customs that were not for the New Testament Christians. In the KJV Paul says, "WHAT came the word of God out of you? Or came it unto you only?" (I Cor. 14:36)

We read in I Corinthians 11:5 when a woman prays or prophecies, she should have her head covered, so women obviously had a part in the church services. Isaiah was married to a prophetess in the Old Testament, so we are sure prophetesses are welcome in the New Testament. Anna was a prophetess at Jesus birth. There is neither male nor female in the body of Christ. (Galatians 3:28)

In Acts 21 we read about Philips four daughters who prophesied. We know Lydia opened her home for a church to meet and was a founding member of the church in Philippi. We see Aquilla and Pricilla working as a team when ministering to Apollos.

James also teaches us not to show preference because of wealth. We are to know one another after the spirit, giving honor to whom honor is due, that includes the leadership that the Lord will raise up among you. The secret of success if to show honor to all who gather together and allow the Holy Spirit to use the talents and giftings in the people the Lord sends your way whether men or women.

Remember South Korea, where the largest church in the world was built through women who began house churches. Lydia, in the New Testament, opened her house for a church to begin in Philippi. Pricilla opened her home for a church. Many women are going to be used in this move of God!

We give special honor to those who are leaders in the church whether they are men or women.

When we tell the world we belong to Jesus, our lives should reflect holy and honorable lives in our homes and businesses as well as when we gather together. As the world comes to an end, and the nearer we come to the return of Christ, the more the church should shine and give hope to hearts that are seeking answers to life.

## CHAPTER NINE
# SOME CHURCH HISTORY

This chapter is a very brief overview of some of the most relevant areas of history of the church when it comes to how the church changed from meeting in homes into a public meeting place for formal worship. The Book of Acts and the Epistles should be our blueprint for meeting as believers. It is foundational that we believe the Bible is our Blueprint and relevant in every area of life.

### *THE BIBLE*

The Bible with its 27-book New Testament canon, as accepted by the Early Christian Fathers, and finally ratified by the Council of Carthage, became, without further questioning, the recognized Bible as God's word. This council met in 397 A.D. Constantine and his Edict of Toleration in 313 A.D. allowed freedom of religion, and before this time there were very few church councils or conferences where Christians from distant parts could come together freely and compare notes on what writings they had. However, there had been an earlier council in 325 A.D. at Nicaea when the recognized church leaders of the council condemned a false teaching called Arianism.

The one criterion by which a book was judged as divine and accepted into the Bible was whether it was of genuine Apostolic origin. Eusebius, A.D. 264-340, bishop of Caesarea, a Church historian, lived through and was imprisoned during Diocletian's persecution of Christians which was Rome's final effort to blot out the

Christian Name. One of Diocletian's objectives was the destruction of all Christian Scriptures. For ten years Bibles were hunted by the agents of Rome and burned in public Market places. (Haley's Handbook.)

However, Eusebius lived through that persecution and came to become Constantine's chief religious advisor. One of Constantine's first acts on ascending the throne was to order, for the churches of Constantinople, fifty Bibles to be prepared under the direction of Eusebius by skillful copyists on the finest vellum and to be delivered by royal carriages from Caesarea to Constantinople.

While records of the early church fathers show that they agreed when they counted the same books as divine and finalized the New Testament cannon at the Council of Carthage in 397 A.D., Eusebius had earlier compiled all of the 27 books that the Council of Carthage agreed on for this earlier project. He was, also a member at the Council of Carthage. In Eusebius' historical account he speaks of four classes of books:

1. Those universally accepted.
2. The disputed books: James, II Peter, Jude, II and III John, which though included in his own Bibles, were doubted by some, and accepted by the Council of Carthage.
3. The spurious books: among which he mentions as the Acts of Paul, Shepherd of Hermas, Apocalypse of Peter, Epistle of Barnabas and Didache.
4. Forgeries of heretics: Gospel of Peter, Gospel of Thomas, Gospel of Mattias, Acts of Andrew and Acts of John. None of these

last two groups were accepted as canon.

We can be assured that the New Testament as we know it is divinely inspired and is Spirit and truth. It is truly amazing to see the hand of God in providing the written word as a means of showing us his eternal plan and deity. We see the Old Testament revealed in the New Testaments revelation of Jesus and His plan for the church. The Lord Jesus confirms the word preached. Mark 16:20. The Holy Spirit and the Word agree!

The New Testament writers refer to the "Scriptures", which is the Old Testament cannon. It is God's plan to use the written word to speak to mankind, and it is confirmed by the Holy Spirit. Jesus is the living expression of the written word of God.

As the writings of the apostles appeared, they were added to the Old Testament writings and were held in the same sacred regard. The canonical New Testament Books were those which came to be generally recognized by the Churches as the genuine and authentic writings of apostolic authority. Archeologists have found more copies or the Scriptures by far than any other writings. The ancient manuscripts do not vary from today other than being transcribed into modern translations. The early scriptures were written in the vernacular of the day. The purpose of the written word is to know HIM! Knowledge puffs up but love builds up. However, that is not an excuse not to learn and study the scripture!

Faith comes by hearing and hearing by the word of God. All that we do and think as believers should be out of a heart to know Jesus and the word better, that we might be obedient to His plan for the church. We will all stand before the judgment seat of Christ and give an account. This should not bring fear, but an excitement and joy that God loves us and desires to reveal to us His plans for the church. If we love Jesus, we will not be deceived, and we will love truth! (II Thessalonians 1:10) John 1:1 Jesus himself is called the Word of God.

## *THE CHURCH*

Church history can be divided into three periods: The first period is the Roman Empire Period. The church was established during the Roman Empire Period. Rome was in power when Jesus was born in Bethlehem of Judea. The Jews were looking for a Messiah to deliver them from Roman rule.

We see persecution, martyrs, the church fathers, controversies, and the Christianization of the Roman Empire during this time despite terrible persecution of Christians by the first eleven Caesars. The zenith of Roman power was from 46 B.C. to A.D. 180. In 70 A.D. the temple in Jerusalem was destroyed.

The decline and fall of the Roman Empire took place from 180-476 A.D. During this time some of the next 17 Caesars tolerated Christians. However, Christians were severely persecuted during the first three centuries.

We want to note that the first church building was erected in the reign of Alexander Severus, 222-235 A.D. who was favorable towards Christianity. It seems during this time of seventeen different Caesars about every other Caesar was favorable toward Christians. However, Diocletian who reigned right before Constantine in 284-305, persecuted Christians furiously.

Following Diocletian, Constantine became Caesar, 306-337 A.D. and he became a Christian himself. By 313 Christians were numbered about one-half of the population of the Roman Empire. After the Edict of Toleration by Constantine they began to build church buildings everywhere. Many reforms took place such as ending slavery, gladiatorial fights, killing of unwelcome children, and crucifixion as a form of execution. These atrocities were abolished because of the influence of the church. Constantine is often said to have made Christianity the national religion, but history tells us he promoted tolerance of all faiths. It was later that Christianity became the national religion under Theodosius, 378-395 who was the last Caesar before the church divided into east and west.

After Constantine, Julian became emperor and he was an apostate, who sought to restore paganism. After him came a Christian, Jovian who re-established the Christian faith and then Theodosius, 378-395, who made Christianity the state religion.

Sadly, when persecution on a large scale stopped, the church of the 4th and 5th centuries became an entirely different institution from the persecuted church of the first three centuries. Worship at first was very simple and the believers met in homes, but during the fourth century the church structure began to be developed into elaborate stately, imposing ceremonies having all the outward splendor that had belonged to heathen temples. Ministers became priests. The term priest was not applied to Christian ministers before 200 A.D. It was borrowed from the Jewish system and from the example of heathen priesthood.

Becoming a political institution was the downfall of Christianity when Theodosius forced conversion and suppressed all other religions. This brought unregenerate people into church paradigm. Under his decrees, heathen temples were torn down by mobs of Christians, and there was much bloodshed. Christ had designed the church to spread His kingdom by purely spiritual and moral means. Conversion to Christianity must be voluntary with a genuine change of heart and life. The nature of the church had mixture of the political spirit and pattern of Imperial Rome.

The Roman Empire divided into the east and west in 395 A.D. The western empire fell in 476 A.D. at the hands of barbarians. Out of the ruins of the western empire emerged the Papal Empire of Rome who ruled the world for one thousand years. This is called the dark ages of history. It was a time of great falling away from the original form of church worship. The Eastern empire fell much later in 1453 A.D. During the time of the barbarians, Constantine had made Constantinople the religious center for the Eastern Empire rather than Rome.

The Second phase of Church history is called the Reformation. We see the reformation come into the world through Martin Luther in Germany, Zwingli in Switzerland, John Calvin from France, and other reformers in the 1500's. The printing press was invented making the Bible more readily available to common people. Johannes Gutenberg invented the printing press which enabled the Bible to be printed. Reformation comes with the Bible being taken to the masses! The power of the Word of God can change history.

The Third Phase of Church history is called the Modern Phase. World missions has been the emphasis of the church in the last three hundred years. We are continuing in reformation until the Lord returns. There have always been Pentecostal believers within and outside of the organized church throughout history. Some of those pockets were during the dark ages, even though they were few. We cannot put God in a box. He looks upon the heart. We can be so thankful that the Word of God has been preserved through the centuries. Also, as we read the Old Testament prophetic books, we can see that God is a God of history and He knows the beginning from the end as to the decisions of man on planet earth.

It is important to remember at the close of the Apostolic age churches were independent one of another, each being shepherded by a board of pastors. (elders, bishops) Later, the main leader came to be called bishop, and others later, were called presbyters. Gradually the jurisdiction of bishop came to include neighboring towns, but we should stick to scripture for our examples. God is a God of order, and how he places leadership and uses leadership should be appointed by the Spirit and it is up to us to recognize what God is doing. We need to appreciate and receive who is ministering in these offices.

It is interesting to study World history and see the impact of the church upon culture throughout the centuries. God truly does bless the nations that submit to His Lordship. We read in Jesus' Sermon on the Mount that true disciples are the salt of the earth and the light of the world.

# AN OUTLINE ON BECOMING A CHRISTIAN

1. Know that God loves you.

   *John 3: 16 "For God so loved the world that He gave His one and only Son, that whosoever believes in Him shall not perish, but has eternal life."*

   *John 10:10 (Jesus speaking) "I came that they might have life and might have it abundantly."*

2. All of us were born in sin and that sin has separated us from God.

   *Romans 3:23 "All have sinned and fall short of the glory of God.*

   *Romans 6:23 "The wages of sin is death."*

3. Jesus Christ is God's only provision for our sin. Through Jesus we can know and experience God's love and plan for our lives.

   *I Peter 1:18, 19 "You were not redeemed with corruptible things, like silver or gold, but with the <u>precious blood</u> of Christ, as of a lamb without blemish and without spot.*

   *John 14:6 Jesus said, "I am the way, and the truth, and the life; no one comes to the Father, but through me."*

4. We must individually receive Jesus Christ as Savior and Lord; then we will experience God's love and plan for our lives. Repentance is turning our lives over to the Lordship of Christ. We are no longer our own, but we live for his purposes for our life. He will come into our lives by the Holy Spirit.

*John 1:12 "As many as received Him, to them He gave the right to become children of God, even to those who believe in His name."*

*Ephesians 2:8 "By grace you have been saved through faith and not of yourselves, it is the gift of God; not as a result of works, that no one should boast."*

*Make a public confession through water baptism.*

---

If you desire to become a Christian, pray this prayer to receive Jesus.

Lord Jesus, I need you. Thank you for dying on the cross for my sins, I open the door of my heart and receive you as my Savior and Lord. I confess that I have sinned, and I thank you for forgiving my sins and giving me eternal life. I give you my life. Make me the kind of person you want me to be. THANK YOU, Jesus for dying on the cross for me.

# AN OUTLINE ON RECEIVING THE HOLY SPIRIT BAPTISM

**Jesus said for you to receive this experience.** It was His last instruction before ascending to the Father.

"Behold, I send the Promise of my Father upon you, but tarry in the city of Jerusalem until you are endued with power from on high." Luke 24:50

"But you shall receive power after that the Holy Ghost is come upon you, and ye shall be witnesses unto me in Jerusalem and in all Judea and Samaria, and to the end of the world." Acts 1:8

John the Baptist, speaking of Jesus, said, "I indeed baptize you with water, but One mightier than I is coming, whose sandal strap I am not worthy to loose. He will baptize you with the Holy Spirit and fire." Luke 3:16

**Examples in the Book of Acts that show the first century church had this experience:**

- On the day of Pentecost - Acts 2:4
- At Cornelius's House - Acts 10:46-48
- The Ephesian believers - Acts 19:6
- The Samaritan's receive - Acts 8:14-17

**What are the requirements to receiving the Baptism in the Holy Spirit?**

- You must be saved - Acts 2:38, 39

- You must receive by faith in Jesus who is the baptizer in the Holy Spirit - Luke 10:10-13, II Cor. 1:20
- You must desire to do the works of Jesus and be his witness - John 14:12

## **Why Tongues?**

A. Tongues are for building you up spiritually.

*"He who speaks in a tongue edifies himself."* I Corinthians 14:4

*"But you, beloved, building yourselves up in your most holy faith, praying in the Holy Spirit."* Jude 20

B. For prayer and intercession.

*"Likewise, the Spirit helps us in our weakness; for we do not know how to pray as we ought, but the Spirit Himself intercedes for us with sighing's too deep for words.* Rom. 8:26

*"For if I pray in a tongue, my spirit prays, but my understanding is unfruitful. What is the conclusion then? I will pray with the spirit, and I will pray with the understanding.* I Cor. 14:14, 15

This was promised through the Old Testament Prophets. Isaiah 28:11, 12, Joel 2:28-32, Psalms 8:2

## **You must ask, believe, and receive:**

This only I want to learn from you: Did you receive the Spirit by the works of the law or by the hearing of faith? Have you suffered so many things in vain, if indeed it was in vain? Therefore, He who supplies the Spirit to you and works miracles among you, does He do it by the works of the law, or by the hearing of faith?" Galatians 3

JESUS IS THE BAPTIZER IN THE HOLY SPIRIT

# TWENTY-NINE EVANGELISM IDEAS THAT WORK

### **Bible Studies**

1. Begin a neighborhood study in your home.
2. Begin a Bible study at a local nursing home.
3. Start and lead a Bible study at work during lunch.

### **Children**

4. Invite and take neighborhood children to church
5. Start a Sunday School class and build it.
6. Start a Bible club with neighborhood kids meeting at your house. (Sermons4Kids on internet)
7. Put on puppet shows at a local park or other public place.
8. Develop a theatre ministry and take it to churches and public places.
9. Develop a children's choir and offer to sing at different events.
10. Help in Vacation Bible School.
11. Volunteer to help at church summer camp.

## **Jails and Prisons**

12. Join a prison or jail ministry team.
13. Become a pen-pal to a prisoner.

## **Books and Booklets**

14. Leave tracts in restaurants
15. Pass out tracts at large public events.
16. Distribute tracts wherever people hand out.
17. Contribute Christian books to your school or public library.
18. Distribute evangelistic books and booklets in nursing homes, or doctor offices, etc.

## **Other Ideas:**

19. Volunteer time at a local mission or other para-church ministry.
20. Do an evangelistic survey door to door.
21. Have a float representing the Lord in your local parades.
22. Be bold and have a street meeting with some friends in a neighborhood park or place people hang out.
23. Enroll in a short-term missionary outreach, either in the U.S. or foreign.
24. Serve on a distress hotline.

25. Train for and be a phone counselor at a local TV station.
26. Have a neighborhood coffee and invite a friend to share her testimony.
27. Write evangelistic letters to the editor of your local newspaper.
28. Invite neighborhood friends in and show a Christian movie or video.
29. Share your testimony at every opportunity.

*Therefore, my beloved brethren, be steadfast, immovable, always abounding in the work of the Lord, knowing that your labor is not in vain in the Lord. I Cor. 15:58*

*The harvest truly is plentiful, but the laborers are few, therefore pray the Lord of the harvest to send out laborers unto His harvest. Matt. 9:37, 38*

*And they went out and preached everywhere that men should repent. Mark 6:12*

# ABOUT THE AUTHOR

My husband, Jerry and I are credentialed with the Assemblies of God. We were a part of the Jesus movement, or Charismatic movement of the nineteen seventies.

It was as new believers that we experienced a vital house church movement that was prompted by the Holy Spirit and believers naturally came together in homes, restaurants, and coffee houses, etc. It was a movement spurred by the Holy Spirit that centered around testimonies of radically changed lives including ours. It was a lay movement, even though the word lay isn't in the Bible.

Our years of ministry include founding Danville Rescue Mission in Danville Illinois and being CEO's of homeless shelters in Indianapolis, IN and Huntsville, AL., tent evangelism, some television radio ministry and pastors of two AG churches in Illinois. We have hosted many outreach meetings in our area through the years, bringing in special speakers and ministries.

It is my hope that believers would take as seriously being obedient to a scriptural form of having church as we do any other doctrine. My prayer is that fresh fire will prompt a new national revival, and a new wine skin will emerge that truly develops the ministry of the every-day Christian as well as bring this nation back to its manifest destiny!

For feedback, licensing, or any other comments, feel free to contact us at Feedback@YowzaPublishing.com.

# House Churches

www.ingramcontent.com/pod-product-compliance
Lightning Source LLC
Chambersburg PA
CBHW031455040426
42444CB00007B/1115